Old BIRMINGHAM EXCURSIONS

by

Eric Armstrong

The Bilberry Tea-rooms at Rednal were a Mecca for parched and hungry day-trippers. The canopy on the right isn't visible in the picture on page 16, and the sender of this postcard has complained about the lack of activity 'on account of so much rain'. What appear to be swing boats at the left of the picture are certainly not swinging.

First published in the United Kingdom, 1999,
by Stenlake Publishing, Ochiltree Sawmill, The Lade,
Ochiltree, Ayrshire, KA18 2NX
Telephone / Fax: 01290 423114

ISBN 1 84033 074 0

ACKNOWLEDGEMENT

The author would like to thank the staff of the Local Studies Department of Birmingham's Central Library for their help during the research of this book.

Between the wars, Sutton Park in Sutton Coldfield was rivalled only by the Lickey Hills as the most popular destination for a day out for Birmingham people. Roughly a quarter of the 2,400 acre park is woodland, and Gum Slade, 'haunt of woodpeckers and nuthatches', with its aged oak trees, is typical of many areas.

For the compiler and his pals, 'a day out at the Lickeys' started by catching a No. 6 tram from its terminus in Perry Barr. The route ran roughly from north to south Birmingham, and entailed a two tram journey - the No. 6 'into town' and the No. 70 from the city centre to Rednal. This picture was taken from the bridge that crosses above Perry Barr railway station. The shop where the lorry has stopped, or one of its close neighbours, is where, at the age of 15, I went each Saturday to collect a bag of a made-to-order bird seed mixture, at the request of a canary and budgie fancier uncle. The following dozen pictures show some of the scenes encountered on the journey to the Lickeys.

Six Ways, Aston, a well-known crossing on the way into town. Six Ways post office (Alma Street) is on the left. The building with the clock is a bank standing at the junction of Lozells Road and Birchfield Road. The No. 6 tram travelled along the tracks running off the near right-hand edge of the picture as it made its way along High Street Aston towards the city centre. Witton Road and Victoria Road lead off to the right, near where the two policemen are standing by the overhead wire standard.

Lancaster Place served as a major crossing point for a variety of tram routes, including the No. 6. The road directly ahead is lower Corporation Street, with the redbrick tower of Central Hall soaring above the traffic on the left. The picture was taken from the new central fire station, built in the 1930s and sorely tested by the blitz of 1940-1941. The terminus for the No. 6 tram was in Martineau Street, which led into Corporation Street. From there it was a relatively short walk to Navigation Street (see picture on the inside front cover) where, with luck, a No. 70 tram would be waiting.

Having travelled through the inner city, the route of the No. 70 ran almost entirely along Bristol Street, Bristol Road, then Bristol Road South before finally reaching Lickey Road. The top hatted driver of this well laden hansom cab is driving his vehicle towards the city centre. Hansoms are named after Joseph Hansom, who as well as inventing the famous cab was one of the architects of Birmingham's town hall.

Fashionable folk bowling along Bristol Road, probably a year or two after the picture opposite was taken. The driver is wearing a long motoring coat and light-coloured hat, plus the once-obligatory motoring gloves. It is open to debate whether he has wandered into the tram lines, or chosen to drive in them. The card was posted in August 1911.

Located in the suburb of Edgbaston, King Edward's Grammar School was one of the landmarks encountered on the Bristol Road. The school moved to Edgbaston in the thirties having previously been situated in New Street. Behind and parallel with the boys' school is King Edward VI High School for Girls.

Birmingham's redbrick university, separated only by Edgbaston Park Road from the King Edward schools, was opened in 1909 by King Edward VII and Queen Alexandra. The playing fields shown run along the back of the Great Hall and stretch down to Bristol Road. Sir Joseph Chamberlain, distinguished Birmingham MP and statesman, was the university's first chancellor, and the clock tower is affectionately dedicated to 'Joe'.

Designed and normally used for official functions, such as degree ceremonies and examinations, the Great Hall served a quite different purpose as a military hospital during World War I. Military order and discipline seem well in evidence in the arrangement of this extra large Nightingale-type ward. Some 67,000 patients had been treated at the makeshift hospital by the end of the war.

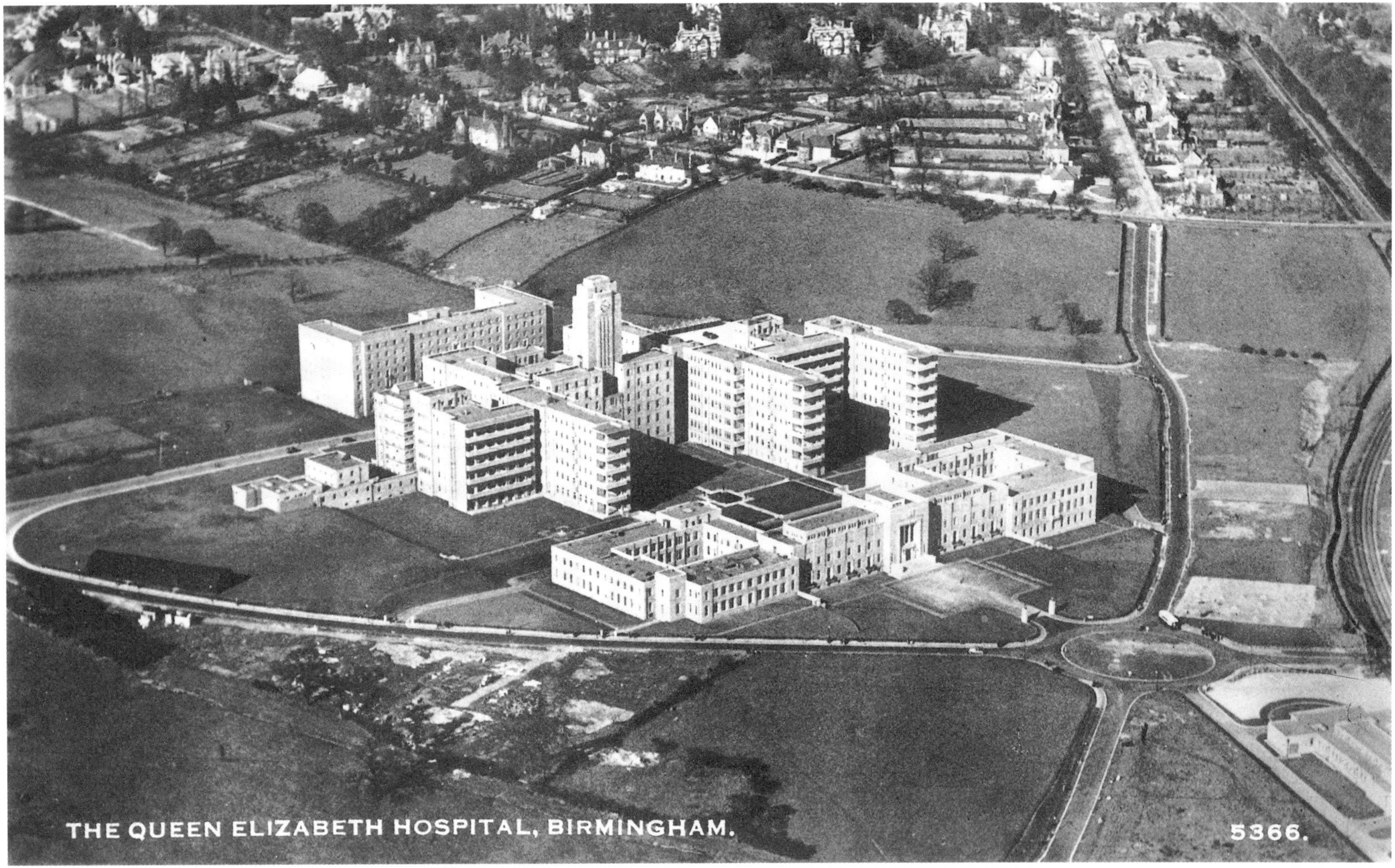

The Queen Elizabeth hospital was built a little to the north-west of the university during the inter-war years, and was opened in 1938 by the Duke of Gloucester. The following year Queen Elizabeth was able to attend the naming ceremony. Large residential properties that typify parts of well-heeled Edgbaston are visible in the background. On the right-hand edge of the card railway lines can just be seen, leading to the city centre and outwards to Bournville, Northfield, Longbridge and beyond. The Worcester & Birmingham Canal runs alongside the railway between the hospital and the university.

On long stretches of Bristol Road, the tram tracks to Rednal and Rubery were carried on a central reservation, opened in the twenties. This enabled trams to maintain good speeds, although also made them sway about - to the slight alarm of some passengers - and drivers had to judge what the acceptable limits of this were. To the left of the lorry is the opening to Whitehill Lane. The fine white house opposite, set in extensive grounds, was once the home of a member of the Cadbury family and was given by him to become a hospital for cripples. This was later converted to become the Royal Orthopaedic Hospital.

This card is one of a series published by Mitchells and Butlers, and shows an aptly-named new pub, with a perhaps less appropriate thatched roof. The Travellers Rest is situated on Bristol Road South between Whitehill Lane and Bell Lane, on the edge of the 'main street' of Northfield. The back of the card bears the M&B slogan - Good Honest Beer - and the firm's widely recognised Deer's Leap trademark, showing a stag bounding across a rocky chasm.

A section of old and new Northfield. Between the wars and again after World War II, as factories opened up or expanded in the area, many new houses were built in Northfield, turning the former village into a dormitory suburb. The Bell Inn was a Davenports house. This brewery made a speciality of their 'beer at home' service, delivering, like milkmen, bottled beers and stouts to the doorstep. The building with the clock stands on the corner of Bell Lane. The Bell Inn was demolished in the early 1980s.

At Longbridge, Bristol Road South (A38) headed off to the right, and at the fork in the road No. 70 trams continued past the Austin works and along Lickey Road to the Rednal terminus. Herbert Austin (1866-1941) opened his Longbridge car factory in 1905. Knighted for his work in producing guns and planes during World War I, he later became 1st Baron Austin of Longbridge. During many years of car production, the factory has been associated with two winners in motoring history, the 'Baby' Austin 7 of the 1920s and the Mini from the 1950s onwards. *14 September 1940. A most successful and enjoyable ramble. Set back at 8 Rednal.* (Air raid) *Warnings went. Had to alight* (from tram) *Walked. Bristol Rd. Miles.'*

A recent publicity brochure describes the Lickey Hills Country Park as 'over 500 acres of deciduous and coniferous woodland, marshy areas and heathland, with a rich variety of wildlife'. For the first fifty years of this century, this attractive corner of Worcestershire served as an invaluable lung, providing fresh country air to many thousands of people. This card was written and posted on 25 July 1913 and reads: 'Dear Joe, this is a photo of the Lickey Hills, we got a motor service to them now. 4d each way, it's grand.'

Once at the Lickeys, refreshments could be bought at the popular Bilberry Tea-rooms. This picture shows a two-way throng of day-trippers moving to and from the tram terminus past the tea-rooms. The wooded countryside provided excellent opportunities for a 'jolly good ramble', 'a spot of courting', or simply a chance to find some solitude. There were stepped paths up the hillside, such as the one on the left, Beacon Hill could be scaled, and on grassy slopes impromptu games of cricket and football were played. If the weather was anything like decent, a few hours at the Lickeys provided a Shangri-La experience for many working class people.

This postcard of Cofton Woods was sent on 4 August 1937 and the message to its recipient, a Mrs Robbins of Hornschurch, reads: 'I never feel I can come to the Lickeys without sending you a card. Really it is a lovely spot. I wonder if ever you will see it. I hope so one day.'

This card was sent to Amsterdam on 20 August 1948 by a Dutch visitor. The well-wooded hillsides illustrate the appeal for ramblers, dog walkers, or those who just want to get away from it all for a bit.

Now largely in the care of the National Trust, the Clent Hills of Worcestershire lie some ten miles to the south-west of Birmingham. Prior to World War II, the most straightforward route to Clent from the city centre would be along Broad Street, Hagley Road, Hagley Road West, through Quinton and towards Hagley village. The greater distance involved and the absence of tram services meant that this beauty spot received fewer Brummie visitors than the Lickeys. This card is postmarked 1906 and together with the following four pictures illustrates a journey to Clent.

Plenty of traffic at Five Ways, Edgbaston at 3.10 p.m., including a single-decker bus bound for Bewdley on the banks of the Severn in Worcestershire. On the corner of Islington Row and Calthorpe Road stands a mansion-style branch of Lloyds Bank. Five Ways originally marked the boundary between Birmingham and Edgbaston. The standing statue is of Joseph Sturge (1794-1859), merchant and Quaker philanthropist, anti-slavery campaigner and pro-adult suffrage Radical.

At stages along Hagley Road, Hagley Road West and beyond to the Clent Hills various well-known hostelries could be patronised. The Plough and Harrow was one of the posher ones.

Situated at a corner of a busy crossroads, this staging post was, and remains, well placed to serve the thirsty traveller. Routes led straight across to Hagley Road West and on perhaps to Clent; left into Lordswood Road, route of the No. 11 bus travelling to Selly Oak and Bournville; and right into Bearwood Road, Smethwick (home to M&B's Cape Hill Brewery).

Before becoming a suburb straddling the western end of Hagley Road, Quinton was an ancient parish. The scene is typical of outer suburban developments built between the wars, with an overall sense of spaciousness, enormous traffic roundabout, shops set well back from the carriageway, generous grass verges, and a giant new pub with good car and coach parking facilities.

The Walton and Clent Hills rise east and north of the village of Clent to a height of just over 1,000 feet. This was a far quieter beauty spot than the Lickeys and one of great charm. The area remains more suited to ramblers than day trippers.

A day out didn't necessarily entail long journeys, and the upmarket residential area of Edgbaston was home not only to the Warwickshire County Cricket Ground, but also to Cannon Hill Park and the Birmingham Botanical Gardens. This picture shows the park's main drive and probably dates from before the First World War. On the lawn tennis courts men are playing in trousers and ladies in long white dresses.

The estate known as Cannon Hill Fields was given to the city of Birmingham by Miss Louisa Anne Ryland in 1873. As extra land was acquired, the area became one of the city's largest parks. Miss Ryland's declared objective was to provide an area of recreation for Birmingham people, and the park has certainly fulfilled that role. Miss Ryland (d.1889), daughter of a wealthy industrialist, never married and gave other tracts of land, which became parks, to the people of Birmingham.

Situated in Westbourne Road, Edgbaston, the Botanical Gardens were planned, laid out and stocked during 1831 by the Scotsman John Claudius Loudon (1783-1843). From an early age Loudon took a keen interest in botany and landscape gardening, working in England and travelling extensively. His work was highly regarded during the Victorian era. He wrote extensively on horticulture and his publications include an Encyclopaedia of Gardening (1822). Recent publicity literature states that 'within the 14 acres of manicured gardens, impressive glasshouses create exotic climates in which rare orchids, palm trees, cacti and unusual rain forest vegetation flourish.'

What appears to be a llama, accompanied by a keeper, has attracted the attention of a group of people on the left.

This purpose-built early Victorian exhibition hall (now demolished) took its name from a Bingley House that had previously stood on the site. As the hall was conveniently located near the city centre, people flocked in their thousands to the exhibitions and entertainments that were held there.

Two stands at what was presumably a food trades exhibition, staged at Bingley Hall. One belongs to a local Birmingham firm, the other to the national custard giant, Birds.

From 1920 onwards the British Industries Fair (BIF) was staged annually to showcase the vast array of products that could be bought from Birmingham manufacturers. Organised by the Birmingham Chamber of Commerce, this trade fair was held at Castle Bromwich on the eastern edge of the city. Publicity literature from 1932 proudly described the fair as 'the largest trade exhibition ever seen in this country', adding that 'the Castle Bromwich buildings probably constitute the largest one-storey permanent exhibition hall in the world'. The BIF buildings were given a new facade in 1952, and the improved entrance is visible in the foreground of this picture. *26 February 1938. Went with A, and A's cousin and A's cousin's boss in his car. Very good at B.I.F. Had plenty of catalogues. 6s 8d worth, Glass Wool and Plywood.'* (A 14 year old schoolboy's haul of freebies. It was just a small piece of plywood!) The BIF ceased to be held in 1957.

In 1926 a new corporation bus route which ran in a circle through the then outer parts of Birmingham's suburbs was introduced. It was officially publicised as the 'Outer Circle Omnibus Service No. 11'. 'See Birmingham's Charming Suburbs by Bus - 25 miles for fifteen pence. Illustrated description of Route and Places of Interest'. Perhaps the most 'charming suburb' travelled through was Bournville, of which Linden Road was an important thoroughfare. On a Sunday family outing, the kids would probably be 'on top' and their parents inside a double decker bus such as the one in the picture.

Passing along Linden Road on a summer Saturday, a glimpse could sometimes be had of a cricket match on the Cadbury playing fields. In 1879 the Quaker brothers George and Richard Cadbury built a brand new factory here on the rural southern edge of the city. The concepts of a 'factory in a garden' and a 'model village' became a reality and the factory was - and remains for the most part - bordered by recreation grounds, tree-lined roads, lawns, gardens, and a village green. Houses, of an advanced design for the time, were built for employees, but landlord and related estate responsibilities were transferred to the Bournville Village Trust which built a social hall, baths, almshouses and other village facilities. Many advertising/PR postcards were published by Cadburys, which remains one of the city's major employers.

Passengers might be lucky and hear the carillon (set of bells) ring out from the bell tower as the No. 11 continued on its circuit. During the 1930s, many young men without cars escorted their young ladies on an outer circle trip as part of the courting ritual. The No. 11 was sometimes referred to as the 'love bus'.

This street scene is typical of many shopping areas once to be found in Birmingham's inner suburbs, but shows an unusual point of interest for Outer Circle passengers - part of Winson Green Prison (right background). The prison was built in 1849.

Dudley was once known as the capital of the Black Country and noted for its iron-making tradition. In the late 1930s it was still something of a novelty for Brummies to visit the new zoo in Dudley close to the ruined castle. One commonly used tram route took the traveller past the Hawthorns, the ground of West Bromwich Albion football club, and through West Bromwich, via Dartmouth Square and Carters Green.

The name Bromwich means 'broom village'. The town was built on what was once broom covered heath, but its later history has long been associated with heavy engineering.

The ruined Dudley Castle (the top of the tower is visible here) dates back to the thirteenth century. It was home to John Dudley, Duke of Northumberland who, in 1553, made his daughter-in-law, Lady Jane Grey, Queen of England - although she was queen for only nine days, after which she was beheaded. The castle stands in spacious grounds on a 180 foot hill.

For its day, Dudley Zoo (located near the foot of the castle) was in the forefront of zoo design. This card (posted in 1938) shows how imaginative use was made of old limestone pits in order to give the lions far more space and fresh air than had customarily been the case at older, more traditional zoos. *25 March 1940. Easter Monday. Extremely interesting and well set out zoo. Wonderful pits for lions, tigers and bears. Sea-lions clever and amusing. Concrete effects very good. Natural surroundings for animals.*

Built to the south-east of Birmingham near the boundary between the city and Solihull, Elmdon airport was well placed to serve West Midlands travellers. Some of the original runways were formed from a special type of grass to reduce damage to aircraft landing wheels and tail skids. From these modest beginnings, a mighty international airport grew. *8 July 1939. Stood in rain from 1/2 past 12 to 1/2 past five but it was well worth it. Excellent aerial display, despite the terrible conditions. Poor attendance. Duchess of Kent, Chamberlain and Crump. Spitfires, Hurricanes, Blenheims, Skuas etc.* This was a unique day out, attending, with girlfriend, the opening of Birmingham's airport. As the three monoplanes in the foreground are two-seaters and carry roundels on their wings, they may well be RAF trainers. The much expanded airport of today has the NEC as its neighbour.

Residents of northern Birmingham suburbs were particularly well placed to visit Sutton Coldfield, where they might window-shop in the town and walk in its spacious park. Although tram routes did not extend from Birmingham into Sutton, local train services were good, special excursions were sometimes arranged and the ever dependable Midland Red buses were rightly popular. This old market town has links with royalty that date back hundreds of years. It was through the influence of a local man, John Vesey (who became Bishop of Exeter in 1519), that Henry VIII granted royal status to the town. Bishop Vesey's name lives on in the grammar school he founded in Sutton. The Parade, with its fine shops and air of prosperity, lies at the heart of the old town.

Sutton Coldfield is principally residential in character and was incorporated into Birmingham in 1974. At its northern end The Parade enters Mill Street (above). The sender of this postcard writes: 'I was at this place on Tuesd. It is a lovely place, there is a very large park with 7 large pools in it . . .' The picture dates from around 1910.

It was because of its 'very large park with 7 large pools' that Sutton attracted many thousands of Birmingham visitors. In 1528, King Henry VIII granted a royal charter to Sutton Coldfield and, as a result, an area known as 'the chase' was given to the townspeople in perpetuity. Now the park, this consists of some 2,400 acres of woodlands, heath and lakes, maintained in an essentially natural condition. Sutton Park can be entered by various gates for a small fee, and this picture shows the main entrance from the town.

Until 1964 there had been a passenger railway station within the park, and this was especially busy at holiday times. My friends and I usually took the No. 29 bus to its terminus at Kingstanding and then trudged up Rough Road to Banners Gate. From there it was no great distance to Longmoor Pool or Powell's Pool.

Between the wars the park was enormously popular at bank holidays, especially if the day was fine, with attendances of up to 60,000 people recorded. For townies, the pools held a particular appeal, notably Keeper's Pool with its outdoor swimming baths. Facilities for swimming had been provided as far back as 1887.

The rustic charm of Bracebridge Cottage and Pool. From time to time the cottage has served as a tea-room. The pool was made in the fifteenth century to stock and supply fish for the table of Sir Ralph Bracebridge.

The pools of Sutton Park provided a variety of different sorts of recreation, including boating and fishing, as well as swimming facilities at Keepers Pool. This picture of Wyndley Pool predates its inclusion in Sutton Park in 1937, and is probably a pre-World War I view. Since the end of World War II, the recreational activities and range of organised events have been greatly expanded. A leisure centre has been built close to Wyndley Pool, cross country and cyclo cross competitions have been held, and cars have raced through the park as part of an RAC rally.

Blackroot Pool apparently derives its name from 'a black root or stump of an oak tree, used for tethering boats, which once stood on a mound in the middle of the pool'. The pool was made smaller when a railway line was built through the park in 1879. The site of a vanished racecourse lies near Blackroot Pool.

As well as woodland, the park also includes extensive tracts of heathland, as the views around Rowton's Well illustrate. It is thought by some researchers that as the derivation of Rowton is 'camp on the hill' the Romans may have used water from the well. The park contains a 1 1/4 mile stretch of the Roman road Icknield Street. *23 August 1940. Helped Mom with the housework a little . . . then went for a ride around Sutton. The park looks lovely with its great sweeps of purple heather and one wonders why the world and its occupants should so suddenly become mad when there are so many beautiful things to behold in life.* A fair enough question and partly a reaction to the recent intense air raids on Brum.

Of the park's seven pools, Powell's Pool is the largest. Over the years Sutton Park has been the location for many celebratory occasions including a pageant in 1928 to commemorate the town's 400 year old charter, the Silver Jubilee of King George V in 1935, and the Coronation of King George VI and Queen Elizabeth in 1937. In 1957 the World Jubilee Jamboree of the Scout movement was held in the park.